The Sick Pets

by Jessica Quilty

Scott Foresman
is an imprint of

PEARSON

Glenview, Illinois • Boston, Massachusetts • Chandler, Arizona
Upper Saddle River, New Jersey

ISBN 13: 978-0-328-50700-9
ISBN 10:   0-328-50700-8

10 V010 15 14 13

Here is Pip.

Pip is sick.

Here is Bix.
Bix is sick.

Here is Vin.

Vin is sick.

Here is the vet.
She can fix up Pip,
Bix, and Vin.

Here is Tim.

What can he do?

Tim can take Vin back.

How to Be a Vet!

Some people who like science and animals want to become vets. People go to school for many years to be vets. There are special schools that teach how to be a doctor for animals. There are thousands of vets in the United States!